W9-BJR-320

NADEN, CORINNE J

THE HAYMARKET
AFFAIR, CHICAGO,
1886

THE HAYMARKET AFFAIR

On May 4, 1886, a riot broke out between workers and police in Haymarket Square, Chicago. As a result of the riot, during which one policeman was killed and six later died, eight men were indicted in what became known as the Great Anarchist trial. Although the men were accused of murder, they were also on trial because they were social revolutionaries who had advocated the overthrow of the government, even with the use of violence. The trial that followed the Haymarket riot became a miscarriage of justice. It set off America's first big red scare and dealt the labor movement in the United States a setback in its quest for recognition and bargaining power.

☆   ☆

PRINCIPALS

AUGUST SPIES, ALBERT PARSONS, SAMUEL FIELDEN, MICHAEL SCHWAB, ADOLPH FISCHER, GEORGE ENGEL, LOUIS LINGG, OSCAR NEEBE, the eight "anarchists" indicted to stand trial for the murder of a Chicago policeman.

CAPTAIN WILLIAM PERKINS BLACK, the defense attorney who fought long and unsuccessfully against a prejudiced judge and jury.

JUDGE JOSEPH E. GARY, in whose court the Haymarket trial was conducted and whose record at the trial showed him to be unjust and strongly prejudiced against the defendants.

JOHN PETER ALTGELD, governor of Illinois, who jeopardized his career by pardoning the three remaining Haymarket trial defendants.

Attention Workingmen!

GREAT

MASS-MEETING

TO-NIGHT, at 7.30 o'clock,

AT THE

HAYMARKET, Randolph St., Bet. Desplaines and Halsted.

Good Speakers will be present to denounce the latest atrocious act of the police, the shooting of our fellow-workmen yesterday afternoon.

Workingmen Arm Yourselves and Appear in Full Force!

THE EXECUTIVE COMMITTEE.

Achtung Arbeiter!

Große

Massen-Versammlung

Heute Abend, halb 8 Uhr, auf dem

Heumarkt, Randolph-Straße, zwischen Desplaines- u. Halsted-Str.

☞ Gute Redner werden den neuesten Schurkenstreich der Polizei, indem sie gestern-Nachmittag unsere Brüder erschoß, geißeln.

☞ Arbeiter, bewaffnet Euch und erscheint massenhaft!

Das Executiv-Comite.

A FOCUS BOOK

The Haymarket Affair

Chicago, 1886

The "Great Anarchist" Riot and Trial

by Corinne J. Naden

Illustrated with photographs

FRANKLIN WATTS, INC.

575 Lexington Avenue   New York, N. Y. 10022

For Dad and Nell

The authors and publishers of the Focus Books *wish to acknowledge the helpful editorial suggestions of Professor Richard B. Morris.*

Photographs courtesy of:
The Bettmann Archive, pages 43, 45
The Library of Congress, cover photo, pages 4, 5, 7, 10

Contents

THE HAYMARKET AFFAIR

The Haymarket Square riot

The Bomb

On a rainy Tuesday evening, May 4, 1886, a group of about three hundred people was gathered in Haymarket Square, in Chicago. Mainly factory workers and their families, they were listening to labor leaders speak against police brutality. For the most part, the crowd was quiet and orderly.

Shortly before ten thirty, a large force of policemen, led by two captains, entered the square. They told the crowd to go home.

Suddenly, and seemingly from nowhere, a bomb exploded. For a moment no one moved. Then the Chicago policemen began to fire their guns into the crowd. Some of the workers also had guns and they fired back. People screamed and ran to get away from bullets and clubs.

The Haymarket riot was over in just a few seconds. It would not be forgotten for years.

When the smoke cleared and the screams ceased, one policeman lay dead; seventy were wounded. Six would later die of their injuries. One worker had been killed, another died later; at least twelve were wounded.

The city of Chicago and the entire country were stunned and outraged. Some people believed that the United States was in danger of all-out revolution. The army was alerted; Chicago citizens formed protection groups. Newspapers condemned all radical thinkers — socialists, communists, anarchists. Foreigners, especially Germans, were damned. And above all came the great cry for revenge. The bomb thrower must be put to death, and all radicals must be punished.

Why? Why did a relatively small incident in Chicago cause such fear and turmoil throughout the entire United States? How could one riot involving a few hundred people bring about (1) what has been called a great miscarriage of American justice; (2) the first big red scare in American history; (3) a new awareness and condemnation of socialism, communism, and anarchism; (4) the near-political death of a respected governor; and (5) a severe setback for the labor movement in the United States?

The Haymarket Square riot did cause all these things — and more. And the story began long before the evening of May 4, 1886.

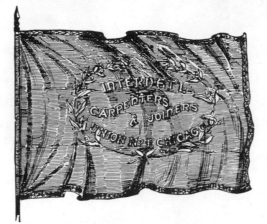

The Labor Movement

The American worker was a restless man in the year 1886. Labor unions were growing in size and strength, and there was hope that an eight-hour working day would become a reality.

Mechanization in the nineteenth century had kept pace with the great population growth by providing increased production in food, clothing, and shelter. But with the expansion in manufacturing, the individual worker began to feel that he had become only a cog in a huge industrial machine.

It seemed natural for workers to band together in unions. They felt that their combined numbers gave them the power to demand and win higher wages and better working conditions from an employer. They also felt that the unions gave them back a certain pride in themselves which they had lost when the machines became so important.

It was also probably natural that the employer did not like the unions very much. If he could get a man to work twelve hours a day, he was not very eager to pay him the same wages for only ten hours

A shoemaker's strike in Massachusetts, 1860

of work. So friction often developed between the unions and the owners. Sometimes there were fights; sometimes there were strikes, even though strikes were illegal.

By the mid-nineteenth century, the economy of the United States was prospering. Workers began to demand a ten-hour day and higher wages. A large number of unions were organized, and in many parts of the country the workingman began to realize some of his demands.

By the 1880's, an American wage earner was far better off than a worker in Europe, but he still had a lot to complain about. The

[4]

average working day was over ten hours. Carpenters earned about $2.42 a day; mill operators $1.24. The average earnings of all American workers in 1883 were just over $1.00 a day.

But the complaints were not only about hours and wages; it was true that salaries were low, but so was the cost of living, and most workers managed to get along fairly well. Often of more concern than wages were the unsafe working conditions and unfair employer practices. The law did very little to protect the worker in these areas. By 1887, for instance, only four states (Massachusetts, New Jersey, Ohio, and Maryland) of the thirty-eight states in the Union at the time had laws that gave the factory worker some protection against fire hazards and poor sanitary conditions. Only four states prohibited the employment of women in the coal mines; only three made it illegal for women to work more than ten hours a day. Only nine states put a restriction on the lowest age for a child to work — he had to be at least ten years old. Twenty states did have some laws about child labor. A child was not allowed to work more than sixty hours a

Lunchtime for New England factory workers

week. Although twelve states had laws about the length of the working day — seven states set the maximum at ten hours, five set it at eight — these regulations were almost meaningless because they were so rarely enforced. The law said an employer could not beat a man if he did not want to work more than the legal number of hours. It certainly did not say that the worker could not be fired for refusing.

In fact, all of the labor laws in the United States in 1886 were inadequate, with so many loopholes that it was very easy for employers to get around them.

Besides being unhappy over the poor protection of the law, workers were also disturbed by some widely used employer practices. One of these was the *blacklist*, a popular device in 1886, and used by employers to keep troublesome workers, especially those involved in union activities, out of work. A list was circulated among business owners; if a man's name was on the list, no one would hire him. Although the blacklist was illegal, use of it was rarely prosecuted, perhaps because most workers did not know that it was against the law.

Other resented practices included the *ironclad oath*, which required a worker to sign a statement that he would not join a union. If he would not sign, he did not get the job. Some workers — and this was especially true of women in the clothing industry — were charged a certain amount of their salaries to pay for the machines they worked on. Other employees were fined for being late to work or for making too much noise or for talking on the job.

All of these conditions and practices made the American worker, in 1886, a restless, unhappy man. He watched his country growing prosperous around him. He was contributing to that prosperity by his labor, and yet he felt that he was not receiving a fair share of the wealth. This was especially true in the large cities, where most of the workers were unskilled.

The city of Chicago was fairly typical of American cities in

[6]

A convention of the Knights of Labor, a powerful labor union in the late nineteenth century

1886. It was growing fast. The population had reached more than 650,000; more than 250,000 were wage earners, many foreign-born. They earned low salaries and had to pay high rents for miserable homes.

Chicago had been the site of labor unrest since 1877 when a large number of workers had gone on strike. The police had tried to break the strike by force. As a result, many strikers had been killed and many more were wounded. The bitter feeling between police and labor still existed nine years later. Many workers were arming themselves for protection.

In the atmosphere of labor unrest in Chicago and the rest of the country European revolutionary ideas spread. Socialist groups, with mainly German members, were established. Their biggest influence was in Chicago and New York City, both of which had a large number of foreign-born workers. Chicago, in particular, had many Germans.

These socialist groups contained elements of anarchism, socialism, and communism. Although there are many extremes of beliefs within each doctrine and some overlapping beliefs among all three, anarchists, in general, oppose any form of government restraint, believing that the individual man, not the government, can best decide what is right or wrong in regard to law. Socialists and communists believe that the workers, through the government, should own the factories and the other means of production.

In 1876, the Workingmen's Party of the United States was formed. A year later it became the Socialist Labor Party of North America. Its aim was to get workers to back socialist candidates, who, in turn, would work to overthrow the capitalist system. Some socialists felt that their goals could be accomplished by political means; others urged the use of violence. In 1881, the platform of the International Working People's Association (I.W.P.A.), formed by ardent revolutionaries, made it clear that physical action in the form of violence, if necessary, was needed to realize its aims.

The American worker in general was not much influenced by the radical philosophies of these organizations. The idea of force was repellent to him and the idea of revolution was foreign. But the city of Chicago became an active center for social-revolutionary thought. This was largely due to the great number of foreign-born, especially German, workers in the city. Socialist beliefs were widely held in Europe and familiar to the Chicago immigrants. Socialist doctrines had become part of organized labor in Chicago, and relations between radical and conservative labor groups were friendly. Therefore, the

[8]

A labor riot in Chicago

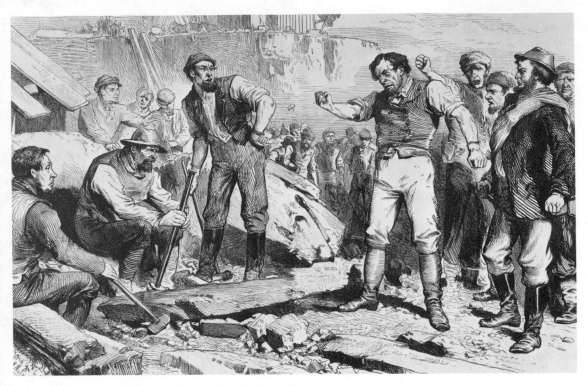
Striking for the eight-hour day

impact of socialist beliefs was probably felt more strongly in Chicago than in any other city in the United States at that time.

Yet even in Chicago, radical thinkers in the labor movement caused little concern to the population as a whole or to political leaders. As elsewhere in the country, in the 1880's, radicals were not regarded in a serious light. Chicago politicians, as well as the Chicago press, looked upon radical groups with something close to amusement. Therefore, unless their activities actually broke the law, these associations were unrestricted in their work.

By 1886, many radicals in Chicago had convinced themselves, for reasons they never explained, that revolution was just around the corner. Private property, regarded as the source of all the evil confronting the workingman, would be abolished. And, if necessary, force would be used to do it.

Also by 1886, the American labor movement as a whole was actively striving for an eight-hour day. The ten-hour day was now fairly common throughout the country. Labor groups believed that a series of strikes affecting national industries would win their goal.

In Chicago, workingmen's organizations named May 1, 1886, as the date for a general strike to gain the eight-hour day.

The Riot

Now that the stage was set for the eight-hour drive, workers in Chicago were particularly enthusiastic. The newspapers and the police force were apprehensive. The whole city seemed tense.

At first the Chicago press had sympathized with the workers' call for a shorter workday. But they had changed their minds when radical thinkers entered the fight, and when the newspapers realized that the workers wanted no decrease in salary for the shorter day.

The Chicago police force, small and overworked, hated by the workingman, was particularly nervous about the May 1 deadline. Since the beginning of the year police had broken up workers' meetings, whether or not the gatherings had been peaceful. Sometimes the workers had struck back, and the friction had steadily increased.

Much trouble had centered around the McCormick Harvester factory, which, because of a dispute over organizing a union, had finally closed its doors on February 16, putting fourteen hundred people out of work. The locked-out workers called a strike two days later. The owner of the factory said he would reopen in March, but that he would hire anyone he pleased. When the plant did reopen, three hundred so-called strikebreakers reported for work.

May 1 came and went. Nothing really happened. There was a general one-day strike and some peaceful parades. Outside of a few minor clashes between workers and police, that was all. Chicago seemed to relax a little.

Two days later some six thousand strikers gathered near the McCormick factory to hear a speech by a socialist newspaper editor named August Spies. The meeting was orderly, and Spies urged the workers to stick together to win their demands.

German-born Spies, thirty-one years old, was a leader in the socialist movement. He had joined the Socialist Labor party in 1877, and accepted violence as a means of realizing labor's goals. Fluent in both English and German, Spies was the editor of a radical party publication called *Die Arbeiter-Zeitung*, which, at the time, had a circulation of about five thousand.

As Spies was finishing his speech, some of the strikers began to leave the group to confront the strikebreakers who were just ending their workday at the McCormick plant. Spies called to the men not to go, but they ignored him. The two groups met and a fight started.

In a short time, two hundred policemen arrived to break up the

REVENGE!

Workingmen, to Arms!!!

Your masters sent out their bloodhounds — the police —; they killed six of your brothers at McCormicks this afternoon. They killed the poor wretches, because they, like you, had the courage to disobey the supreme will of your bosses. They killed them, because they dared ask for the shortenin of the hours of toil. They killed them to show you, "Free American Citizens", that you must be satisfied and contended with whatever your bosses condescend to allow you, or you will get killed!

You have for years endured the most abject humiliations; you have for years suffered unmeasurable iniquities; you have worked yourself to death; you have endured the pangs of want and hunger; your Children you have sacrificed to the factory-lords — in short: You have been miserable and obedient slave all these years: Why? To satisfy the insatiable greed, to fill the coffers of your lazy thieving master? When you ask them now to lessen your burden, he sends his bloodhounds out to shoot you, kill you!

If you ar men, if you are the sons of your grand sires, who have shed their blood to free you, then you will rise i your might, Hercules, and destroy the hideous monster that seeks to destroy you. To arms we call you, to arms!

Your Brothers.

The "Revenge" Circular

struggle. Some shots were fired on both sides, and when it was over, one striker was dead and six were wounded.

Spies, who had tried again to stop the fight, left before it was over to write an editorial for his paper. When the Chicago *Daily News* reported — falsely — that six strikers had been killed, Spies believed it. Outraged, he wrote what came to be known as the "revenge" circular.

Printed in both English and German, the circular informed workingmen that six strikers had been killed because they wanted a shorter workday. It declared that the workers had long endured humiliation and injustice, and that the time had come to rise up and destroy "the hideous monster that seeks to destroy you."

Spies later maintained that he had entitled the circular "Workingmen! To Arms!" But when it was printed, a typesetter had inserted the word "Revenge!" at the beginning of the title. It would prove a fatal mistake for Spies.

Chicago newspapers contributed to the tension. They claimed

that the fight had been caused by "anarchist" agitators. They called the crowd "liquor-crazed."

On the morning of May 4, 1886, Chicago was in an ugly mood. Workers were bitter against the police for the events of the day before, and there were numerous clashes between the two sides throughout the day. The police were tense and braced for trouble. The newspapers continued to blame radical agitators for the unrest.

Labor unions decided to hold demonstrations that night to protest what they called police brutality. Many meetings were planned, but the largest was to be held in Haymarket Square, and it was there that August Spies was to speak.

There is no Haymarket Square today in Chicago, but, in 1886, it was a long rectangle between Desplaines and Halstead streets, partly enclosed by factories and warehouses. It had enough space to hold about twenty thousand people. Nearby was the Desplaines Street Police Station.

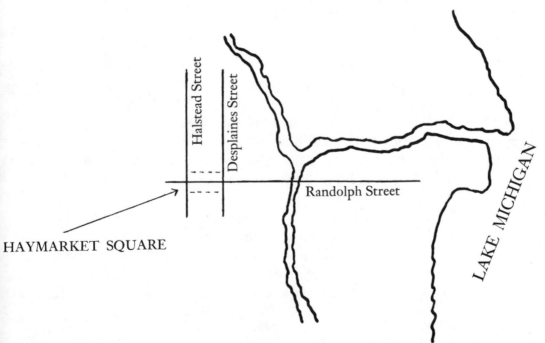

August Spies arrived in Haymarket Square about 8:30 P.M. Although many Chicago labor leaders had armed themselves, Spies did not carry a gun. For about twenty minutes he spoke to a small crowd from the top of a truck wagon. He did not advocate violence. He denied causing the trouble at the McCormick plant the day before (the newspapers had named him as one of the chief instigators), and he blamed the violence on the police and on the employers.

Before his speech, Spies had sent his brother Henry and two young men, Rudolph Schnaubelt and Ernest Legner, to locate Albert Parsons, who was scheduled as the next speaker.

At about 9 P.M., Parsons arrived and began to speak.

Albert R. Parsons, then in his late thirties, was a recognized leader of the revolutionary movement. He had been born in Alabama; had fought for the Confederacy at the age of thirteen; had been the assistant assessor for the United States Internal Revenue in 1870 and the secretary of the Texas State Senate in 1871. He had come to Chicago in 1873, and three years later was a confirmed socialist. In 1877 Parsons had been blacklisted for two years. He was a polished speaker, and very active in politics. He was also editor of *The Alarm*, a party publication which praised anarchist beliefs.

Parsons spoke for about an hour to a crowd of some twelve hundred people. The point of his speech was that socialism was the cure for labor's grievances. He told the crowd that under the capitalist system, a workingman received only fifteen cents of every dollar. He said that although he did not intend to incite anyone to violence, the time had come for the American worker to arm himself if he would gain liberty and justice.

When Parsons had finished his speech, he gave the floor to Samuel J. Fielden, the last speaker. The English-born Fielden, who was close to forty years old, had come to the United States in 1868. His knowledge of socialism and anarchism was not profound, but he was a passionate orator. His talk mainly concerned the inadequate

[16]

protection the law gave to the workingman. The law would not protect the worker, he argued, and, therefore, the worker must protect himself.

He had been speaking for only about ten minutes when it started to rain, causing many people to leave. Fielden kept talking to the three hundred who were left.

At nearly 10:30 P.M., about one hundred and eighty policemen burst into the Square and headed for the wagon where Fielden was speaking. The police were led by Captains John Bonfield and William Ward. Captain Ward told the crowd to leave peacefully. Fielden and the others standing on the wagon began to climb down.

At that moment a dynamite bomb was thrown. With a shattering roar, it exploded near the front line of policemen. At first, there was stunned silence in Haymarket Square.

Then the police began to fire. Some of the strikers fired back. Clubs swung through the air and people tried frantically to get away. The Haymarket riot lasted only a few seconds.

When it was over, one policeman — Mathias J. Degan — was dead, having been killed almost instantly. Degan was thirty-five years old and had joined the force in 1884. Seventy policemen were wounded; six would later die of their injuries. One worker was killed, another died later. At least twelve were wounded.

The Haymarket riot was over. The trouble had only begun.

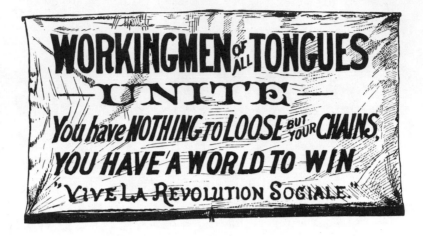

The Trial

Immediately after the Haymarket Square riot, Chicago and the entire country had been stunned. Then fear and anger set in, and the red scare began.

Newspapers gave many false accounts of the riot, thus aggravating the already present fear that more riots were about to break out. Leaving no doubt as to who, in their opinion, was responsible for the bomb, many reporters began their stories with such statements as "The anarchists of Chicago . . . threw a bomb into the midst of policemen. . . ." *The New York Times* spoke of anarchists as being responsible for the bomb, and labeled the act murder. Little mention was made of the casualties among the workers, and the press spoke as one voice in denouncing radicals and holding such leaders as Spies and Parsons responsible for instigating a riot.

In this atmosphere of intense emotion and fear, it was easy for the average citizen to believe that socialists or anarchists were responsible for the bomb. And from this fear grew a cry for revenge — death to the bomb thrower and punishment for the radicals! The very foundations of the United States seemed in danger. Radical thinkers had been given too much leeway in this country, people said. They must be suppressed before they brought about a revolution. Fear seemed to have replaced any logical thinking.

The red scare manifested itself in many ways. The color red was left out of advertisements; foreigners in general, and Germans in particular, were damned, because many of the socialist groups were largely composed of aliens. Organized labor quickly condemned the bomb throwing, as if to get away from the surge of criticism against labor that began to sweep the country. Some Chicago citizens planned to organize vigilante groups as a defense against the coming "revolution." The 1st Infantry Regiment was alerted. Chicago Mayor Carter H. Harrison ordered police to break up all crowds or processions of any kind. Nearly seventy thousand dollars were quickly collected for the dependents of the dead policemen.

A cry for revenge called for swift action. Two days after the riot, Chicago police had brought in over two hundred "radicals" as suspects. Thirty-one were finally indicted on May 27, but most of them became state witnesses or were released on bail. On June 21, 1886 — six and a half weeks after the Haymarket riot and five days after the seventh policeman had died as a result of injuries sustained in the riot — eight men stood trial for the murder of policeman Mathias Degan.

The eight accused were August Spies, Albert Parsons, Samuel Fielden, Michael Schwab, Adolph Fischer, George Engel, Louis Lingg, and Oscar Neebe. They were charged with being accessories to Degan's murder by means of a bomb; with murder by pistols; with being accessories to one another in the murder; and with general conspiracy to murder.

Why those charges and why those men?

The prosecution's charges were based on an Illinois law which made anyone who aided, abetted, or encouraged a crime an acces-

Rudolph Schnaubelt

sory, to be punished accordingly, whether or not the principal person in the crime was ever caught and/or punished. The state did not
say that any of the eight men had thrown the bomb, but if they were
found to be accessories, they could be punished just as though they
had.

The state did assert that the young German radical Rudolph
Schnaubelt was the man who had thrown the bomb, and a witness
was produced to prove the charge. However, during the trial the
witness's story proved unreliable, and the identity of the bomb
thrower is unknown to this day. Schnaubelt disappeared after the
riot, adding to the theory that he was the guilty one. He was never
found. (When the trial opened, Parsons was also missing but he gave
himself up on the afternoon of the twenty-first.)

In order to prove a conspiracy, the result of which was the riot and bomb throwing, the state tried to show that a meeting held by the I.W.P.A. the night before the riot — which the state called the Monday night conspiracy — was called for the purpose of planning the riot. Also important to the state's case was the word "revenge" in Spies's circular. The state contended that this was proof of plans for violent action.

The prosecution also wished to prove that the eight men were enemies of the state as well as accessories to murder. In fact, the attitude of the general public was that this trial would be an example to all those with "revolutionary thoughts."

The specific evidence against August Spies was the revenge circular, and the testimony of the witness who said Schnaubelt had thrown the bomb. At the trial, this witness said that Spies had provided the match to light the fuse. But the witness gave so many versions of his story that he could not be considered reliable. Of course, Spies's reputation as a radical who believed in the use of force was also considered to be evidence against him.

Besides being an important socialist leader, Albert Parsons had long called for using dynamite, if necessary, to gain labor's ends. Yet Parsons had been out of town on May 3 when the so-called secret meeting was held, and he had already left Haymarket Square by the time the bomb was thrown.

Samuel Fielden had not known about the Monday night meeting, but the police testified that he fired a gun at them during the riot. Other witnesses testified that he did not. Fielden swore that he never owned or carried a gun.

Michael Schwab, twenty-nine, was implicated because a witness said that he was with Spies and Schnaubelt before the bomb was thrown. But Schwab claimed that he had left Haymarket Square before the bomb was tossed and had not talked to either Spies or Schnaubelt. Schwab was on the editorial staff of the *Arbeiter-Zeitung*.

[21]

He had come to the United States from Bavaria, and by 1879 was an active socialist.

Adolph Fischer, thirty-seven, was born in Germany, where he became interested in socialism. He also worked at the *Arbeiter-Zeitung*. The evidence against him was that he had attended the Monday night meeting and that he was carrying a gun when he had been arrested. Although he had attended the Haymarket meeting, he was not there when the bomb was thrown.

George Engel was at home when the bomb had exploded. The evidence against him was mainly that he had been present at the Monday night "conspiracy." Engel was fifty years old and had come from Germany in 1873. He had become a socialist when he went to Chicago a year later.

Louis Lingg was not at the Monday night meeting nor in Haymarket Square. But he was a fanatic socialist and he did make dynamite bombs. A witness who lived in Lingg's rooming house testified that Lingg had been making bombs for about six weeks before the Haymarket riot. At twenty-two, German-born Lingg was the youngest of the eight accused, and had come to Chicago only the year before.

Oscar Neebe was thirty-six years old and a not very ardent student of socialism. Born in New York of German parents, he had come to Chicago when he was fifteen and had entered the labor movement in 1875. The evidence for the charge of murder against him was that he belonged to the I.W.P.A.; that he told someone on May 3 that it was about time the workers get their chance; that he owned two dollars' worth of stock in the company which owned *Arbeiter-Zeitung*; and that police found a pistol, a red flag, and a sword in his home when it was illegally searched on May 7.

Of the eight men on trial, six were foreign-born and only two — Parsons and Fielden — were not of German birth or descent.

As lawyers for the defense, the Central Labor Union of Chicago

Left, State's attorney Julius S. Grinnell; right, defense attorney William Perkins Black

had retained two young and relatively inexperienced men, Moses Salomen and Sigismund Zeisler. But a more experienced lawyer was needed. A Chicago doctor and socialist, Ernst Schmidt, organized a defense committee to raise money for a lawyer. In the general atmosphere surrounding the trial, no lawyer was anxious to take the job. However, Captain William Perkins Black, a liberal corporation attorney and gifted orator with a reputation for honesty, consented to head the defense. He was joined by William A. Foster, an Iowa lawyer with some criminal-law experience.

Black immediately asked that the trial—scheduled for the court of Judge John Rogers—be transferred. He charged that Rogers had already shown prejudice in the grand-jury hearings. Black wanted the trial held in the court of Judge Murray Tuley. However, the State's attorney — Julius S. Grinnell — objected, and the trial was transferred instead to the court of Judge Joseph E. Gary.

Perhaps it would have been impossible under the circumstances to secure a fair trial anywhere, but this change of courts proved a fatal blow to the accused men. For although Gary had enjoyed

Judge Joseph E. Gary

a reputation for being an unbiased man until this time, at the Haymarket trial he was unjust and highly prejudiced against the defendants.

This was immediately evident in the selection of the jury. The trial took forty-nine days; twenty-one were spent in picking a jury. Nine hundred and eighty-one citizens were examined. Time and again, Judge Gary failed to disqualify prospective jurors even though they admitted that they had already formed opinions about the case. He failed to disqualify one man who was related to one of the dead policemen, and he qualified another who was a close friend of one of the deceased. He had no objections to one who frankly admitted that he doubted if anyone could change his mind about the guilt of the accused.

Naturally, the defense had a chance to disqualify — called a peremptory challenge — any man for such reasons. Each defendant had twenty peremptory challenges; thus the defense as a whole had

The "Great Anarchist" trial

Harry T. Sandford   Frank S. Osborne   James H. Brayton

Geo. W. Adams   Scott G. Randall   Andrew Hamilton

a total of one hundred and sixty. However, these were quickly used up, and the defense lawyers could only hope that they had secured, not an unbiased jury but at least twelve men who were a little less prejudiced than the other candidates.

The twelve men finally selected were:

George W. Adams, twenty-seven, a traveling salesman for a Chicago paint firm;

James H. Brayton, forty, principal of the Webster School in Chicago;

Chas. B. Todd

John B. Greiner

James H. Cole

Alanson H. Reed

Theo. E. Denker

Chas. H. Ludwig

James H. Cole, fifty-three, a major with the 41st Ohio Infantry during the Civil War. Until just before the trial he had been a book-keeper with a Chicago insurance company;

Theodore E. Denker, twenty-seven, a shipping clerk and a resident of a Chicago suburb;

John B. Greiner, twenty-five, a stenographer with the Chicago and Northwestern Railway;

Andrew Hamilton, a Chicago hardware dealer;

Charles H. Ludwig, twenty-seven, bookkeeper for a Chicago firm;

Frank S. Osborne, thirty-nine, the foreman of the jury. He was a salesman for Marshall Field and Company, a large Chicago department store;

Scott G. Randall, twenty-three, a salesman for a seed company;

Alanson H. Reed, forty-nine, a member of a Chicago firm;

Harry T. Sanford, twenty-five, a clerk with the Chicago and Northwestern Railway; and

Charles B. Todd, forty-seven, a former soldier with the 6th New York Heavy Artillery, and a Chicago salesman.

Of these twelve jurors, only one — Andrew Hamilton — was foreign-born; none was an industrial worker; six were in their twenties; four admitted to a prejudice against radicals; and all admitted to having formed an opinion about the case before the trial.

The Verdict

The state presented its case first. Witnesses testified that Schnaubelt had thrown the bomb, that the defendants had encouraged him,
that one of them had actually made the bomb, and that the violence
in Haymarket Square had been planned at the Monday night meeting. The Haymarket bomb was said to be as great an act of treason
as the firing on Fort Sumter (signaling the start of the Civil War).
Parsons was charged with encouraging the use of dynamite; Spies
with encouraging the use of force through his revenge circular
and with intentionally inciting the riot at the McCormick factory;
Lingg with making the bomb that exploded in Haymarket Square;
and Engel with devising the plan for using the bomb. All eight men,
the prosecution charged, were, to one degree or another, responsible
for the Haymarket crime.

Judge Gary allowed the state to present as evidence the activities
of the defendants for the past three years, even though such testimony had nothing to do with the charges. It did, however, serve to
inflame a public already outraged at the actions of the radicals. This

testimony, the state argued, showed that these men had long been part of a conspiracy to begin a social revolution, and that the plans for that revolution had been drawn up on the evening of May 3 at the I.W.P.A. meeting.

But it was never proven that a revolution had, in fact, been planned on the night of May 3. Two prosecution witnesses, both engaged in socialist activities, testified that at the I.W.P.A. meeting Engel had presented a plan to organize the armed units of workers in the city "in case of emergency." Although this was damaging evidence, the witnesses also admitted, under cross-examination, that nothing was said at the May 3 meeting about Haymarket Square, nor was there any talk of dynamite or bombs. Therefore, it was not shown that Engel's plan on Monday night had any relationship to what happened in Haymarket Square on Tuesday.

It was never proven that Spies's circular was intended to incite the workers to violence. Spies testified that the word "revenge" was inserted without his knowledge. But whether or not that was true, the state could not demonstrate the connection between the revenge circular and the Haymarket riot. In fact, neither side gave any explanation of why the word was inserted.

It was never proven that Lingg made the particular bomb that was thrown in Haymarket Square. Experts for the state could only testify that the bomb that exploded in the Square and the bombs that Lingg made in his home contained similar metal and nuts.

It was never proven that Schnaubelt did throw the bomb. The witness Harry Gilmer testified that he was at the Haymarket meeting and had seen Schnaubelt throw the bomb and Spies light the fuse. However, Gilmer had given a different version of his story to the newspapers. In the first version he did not mention Spies at all, and he described Schnaubelt incorrectly. Thirteen witnesses for the defense swore that Spies never left the wagon from which he had addressed the crowd, and so he could not have lit the bomb fuse.

[30]

The so-called Monday night conspiracy

Gilmer said that Schnaubelt had thrown the bomb from an alley off the Square. Sixteen witnesses swore that the bomb was not thrown from the alley, but south of it. Another state witness said that Schwab had been with Spies and Schnaubelt when the bomb was thrown. But Schwab was able to account for his actions on May 4, and to at least present a reasonable doubt that he was in the Square when the bomb had been thrown.

The state was able to prove, however, that each of the eight accused men was, in fact, engaged in socialist activities.

The defense was largely aimed at denying the charges of the state. Black said that the state had played upon the prejudices of the jury and had used irrelevant material. These men should not be judged for their social beliefs, he argued, but on whether or not they had committed murder. In closing, the defense lawyers declared that if it could not be proven that on May 3 these eight men had entered into a conspiracy to commit murder, then they could not be found guilty of Degan's murder on May 4. And *that* murder was the only crime they were legally being tried for.

All that now remained before the verdict was Judge Gary's charge to the jury. At no other point, except during the selection of jurors, were Gary's decisions more damaging to the eight defendants.

When a judge charges a jury, he gives instructions which the jurors must follow in coming to a verdict. The state asked Gary to give certain charges, and it has been said that these charges greatly affected the outcome of the trial.

Among the charges that the judge allowed were:

(1) that a person could be charged with murder even though he was not at the murder scene and even though the actual murderer was unknown and at large, so long as the person charged and the murderer had been in a conspiracy. (Yet, as the defense argued, since it had not been proven who threw the bomb, how could the defendants be proven to be in a conspiracy with an unknown person? That

[32]

is, how can an "unknown" person be *proven* to be a part of a conspiracy?)

(2) that a person could be held for a crime resulting from a conspiracy to overthrow the state or country, even if he did not commit the crime but was only part of the conspiracy. (But, as the defense argued, it had never been proven during the trial that the eight men were, in fact, part of a conspiracy to overthrow the state or country.)

(3) the most damaging charge of all — that general advice to the public about violent deeds makes the speaker who gives the advice responsible if the deeds are committed. For instance, John Doe tells a gathering that he thinks a certain group of people should be destroyed, but he does not say how or when and he does not name any one person in particular. Someone then murders a few people in that certain group. Even though it cannot be proved that the murderer even heard Doe's speech, Doe can be held responsible as an accessory to murder. (From there it was easy to say that if the accused men ever, at any time, spoke in favor of using violence, then they could be held responsible for the violence that resulted in murder at Haymarket Square.)

Judge Gary refused to give the jury certain charges requested by the defense. These were, among others: (1) a conspiracy must be proven beyond a reasonable doubt in order to find a defendant guilty of murder, and (2) for a man to be guilty of being an accessory it must be shown that he actually aided the one who committed the crime.

The "great anarchist" trial went to the jury on Thursday, August 19, 1886. The police had been alerted in case of trouble. The jurors delivered their verdict with great speed — at 10 A.M. the next morning. August Spies, Albert Parsons, Samuel Fielden, Michael Schwab, Adolph Fischer, George Engel, and Louis Lingg were found guilty of murder, the penalty being death. Oscar Neebe was

[33]

also found guilty of murder, but his penalty was fifteen years in the penitentiary.

The defense lawyers were obviously shaken by the speed of the decision. The defendants were stunned — Neebe perhaps more than any of the others. The evidence linking him with the Haymarket Square riot and Degan's death had been so slight and inconclusive that many people, Neebe included, had expected his release.

But to others the verdict was popular, justified, and satisfying. Crowds cheered, Chicago relaxed, and newspapers all over the country praised the outcome. Anarchism was dead in the United States, they said. Although some labor papers did criticize the verdict, labor as a whole — perhaps through fear of public opinion — was not solidly behind the condemned men.

The defense moved for a new trial, and presented their arguments before Judge Gary on October 1, 1886. They charged that the men had not been proven guilty of murder and that neither the jury nor the press had been impartial.

On October 7, Gary denied the motion. No one had seriously believed that he would do otherwise.

August Spies

Left, Michael Schwab; right, Oscar Neebe

Before a sentence is pronounced, it is customary for the court to ask the defendant if he wishes to state any reasons why the sentence should not be given. From October 7 to 9, the eight men stated their reasons.

August Spies was the first to speak. A handsome, intelligent man, he spoke easily and sincerely. He said that the charge of a conspiracy to overthrow the government was absurd. Although he did not deny his anarchist beliefs (he used socialist and anarchist to mean the same thing), he said that he was being condemned for them and not for murder.

Michael Schwab was next. Not as fluent a speaker as Spies, he was honest, direct, and bitter. He defended his beliefs and protested his innocence. He gave the appearance of a scholarly man although he was not as thorough a student of socialism as Spies.

Oscar Neebe was a colorless personality, although physically powerful, and he knew little of the socialist philosophy. His short, simple talk was moving in its bewilderment. He spoke of the slight

[35]

Left, Louis Lingg; right, Adolph Fischer

evidence against him, and said he was sorry not to be hanged with the others.

The tall, pleasant-looking Adolph Fischer denied his guilt and was passionate in his defense of his views. Fischer was not distinguished as an intellectual. He would sacrifice himself for the cause, he said, but he maintained that the verdict would start the spread of anarchism throughout the country.

Louis Lingg was fanatically dedicated. With great scorn, he told the court that he could be threatened with hanging for his views but that he would never change them. A small, handsome man, he spoke in German with great drama and passion.

George Engel gave the appearance of anything but an ardent revolutionary. Explaining again that he was at home when the bomb was thrown, he denied his guilt and defended his philosophy.

In a long speech, Samuel Fielden protested his innocence and spoke of his beliefs and the evils of capitalism. Fielden was a mild man with a long black beard, but he delivered a speech in a striking manner.

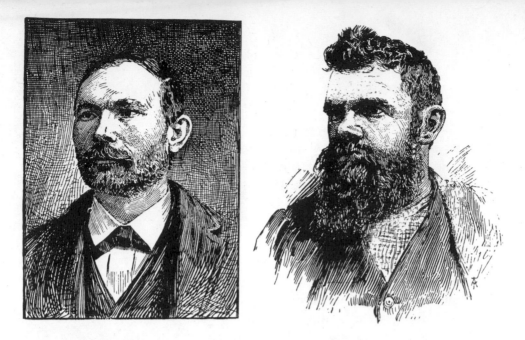

Albert Parsons spoke last and longest — for a total of eight hours. A true leader of socialist causes, he was a most impressive speaker and a dedicated revolutionary. He told the court that he had given himself up because he was innocent. He said that he had broken no laws, and that to carry out the sentences would be judicial murder. He, too, said he was being tried for his views and not for the Haymarket bomb.

Top left, George Engel; top right, Samuel Fielden; bottom, Albert Parsons

When Parsons was finished, Judge Gary addressed the court. He said that liberty and free speech do not entitle a man to use force or dynamite to gain his ends. Then he sentenced Neebe to fifteen years at hard labor in the state penitentiary at Joliet, Illinois. The remaining seven men were sentenced to be hanged between 10 A.M. and 2 P.M. on December 3, 1886.

Captain Black now appealed to the Illinois State Supreme Court. The hearing was set for March 13, 1887, and a stay of execution was granted.

Both the state and defense argued their cases for three days before the six elderly men who made up the court. The defense argued that the trial was unfair and that the defendants had not been found guilty of the crimes as charged.

The court did not reach a decision until September 14, 1887. Unanimously, it upheld the convictions. Only one man, Justice Mulkey, voiced some misgivings about the verdict, even though he voted for it. Once again, popular opinion, encouraged by the press, endorsed the decision.

Now Captain Black had one more legal step open to him — the United States Supreme Court. On October 27, 1887, the defense argued its case before the Court. On November 2, Chief Justice Waite gave the unanimous decision. The nation's highest court would not overrule the lower courts. (In fairness, it must be said that the Supreme Court probably did not interfere with the lower courts because the Haymarket trial did not raise any federal issue.)

The last legal hope for the defendants was gone.

Although newspapers applauded the verdict, public opinion had slowly begun to change by the end of 1887, and so had the attitude of organized labor.

Labor unions had wanted to dissociate themselves from the Haymarket affair because they were afraid that the trial would affect the drive for an eight-hour day. They felt that to become identified with radicals would give the management side another pretext to attack them. But they soon discovered that management was using the bomb to condemn all of labor anyway.

Belatedly aware that a miscarriage of justice was being carried out, labor groups now petitioned Illinois Governor Oglesby to grant pardons to the men. The Progressive Labor party urged workers to protest the verdict in mass meetings throughout the country.

Meanwhile, other liberal citizens began to work for the release of the eight men, as did socialist groups, and an organization known as the Amnesty Association, which had been formed after the trial. This group circulated petitions asking the governor to change the death sentences to life imprisonment. Some public officials, lawyers, and judges signed the petitions. The Amnesty Association also asked the condemned men to sign letters of repentance, which would be sent to the governor. The association felt that this tactic would surely induce Governor Oglesby to change the sentences. But only Spies, Schwab, and Fielden agreed to sign.

The governor was now besieged with pleas to change the sentences or to pardon the men. Some of the petitions were sent from Europe. Chicago once again became a tense, anxious city as it waited for the governor to make up his mind. Rumors circulated that anarchists were planning a jail break to free their comrades.

To those who were working for a favorable decision, a faint ray of hope began to show itself. Surely the governor could not ignore all these requests for leniency.

The ray of hope disappeared on Sunday, November 6, when four six-inch bombs were found in Lingg's cell. Although the size of the bombs seemed to indicate a suicide attempt and not a jail break, the mere fact that they were there swayed public opinion away from the men. Lingg claimed that he did not know how they got in his cell, and the mystery was never solved.

Four days later, Lingg did commit suicide in his cell by placing

[39]

a small dynamite cap in his mouth and lighting it. Although half of his face was blown away, he lived for a number of hours.

How much the finding of the bombs and Lingg's suicide affected the governor's decision is unknown, but that evening Oglesby delivered his verdict. He changed the sentences of Fielden and Schwab to life imprisonment. The other sentences would remain as pronounced. He explained that he considered Fielden and Schwab as not really anarchists and essentially "good" persons at heart.

At 12:15 P.M., November 11, 1887, August Spies, Albert Parsons, Adolph Fischer, and George Engel stood on the gallows, composed and calm. The death sentences were read, nooses were placed about the necks of the four men, and they were hanged.

Liberty or Death!
Adolph Fischer
Cook-Co-Jail
Nov 11th '87.

The Pardon

In 1892, John Peter Altgeld was elected governor of Illinois on the Democratic ticket. Almost immediately he began receiving petitions urging the pardon of the three remaining Haymarket trial defendants — Fielden, Neebe, and Schwab.

Altgeld had an outstanding reputation in the state and country. Born in Germany on December 30, 1847, he came to the United States with his parents when he was three months old. He was brought up on a poverty-ridden farm near Mansfield, Ohio, under the watchful eye of a stern and bigoted father. With no formal schooling, young Altgeld ran away to join the Civil War with the Ohio Home Guards when he was sixteen. After he returned one hundred days later, he went not to the farm but to elementary school.

The young man worked his way around the country doing various jobs. He was a farmhand and teacher in Missouri, a railroad worker in Arkansas. In his spare time he studied law and was admitted to the bar in 1871 at the age of twenty-four. In 1875, he moved to Chicago where he set up a small practice.

John Peter Altgeld

The next few years were busy ones for the young lawyer. He married schoolteacher Emma Ford. He saved money and bought land in Chicago, finally becoming a builder on the side. He wrote a book on the penal system, which he believed *made* criminals instead of reforming them. And he became the partner of famed lawyer Clarence Darrow.

In 1886, Altgeld was elected a judge of Cook County Superior Court, with the backing of Democrats and the United Labor party. Among other lawyers, he was quick to condemn the injustice of the Haymarket trial.

In 1890, he became chief justice of the Cook County Superior

[43]

Court, a position he held for one year before retiring to his law practice once again. Now a millionaire through his real-estate holdings, he published another book, this one on politics and the law.

The Illinois Democratic party needed the perfect candidate for governor in 1891. No Democrat had ever won the governorship, but this seemed the year for reform. Everyone was angry at something: workers at big business; farmers at railroads; liberals at social conditions. Someone had to bring these groups together, and Altgeld became the man. (It was also no hindrance that he could afford to pay for his own campaign.)

Altgeld won the election, and was inaugurated on January 10, 1893, as the first Democratic governor of Illinois, the first foreign-born governor, and the first governor from Chicago. The new governor had earned the reputation of being a thoroughly honest man, and one who was unafraid to voice his true convictions. When he asked for the Haymarket trial records, it was known that he looked upon the pardoning power of a governor as not a personal reward but as a legal responsibility.

The end of the Haymarket trial had not, as many had predicted, brought an end to radical activities in Chicago. On the contrary, for a while they seemed more energetic than before. The Chicago police had also been energetic in shaping up their own ranks, and Captain Bonfield, who had led his men into Haymarket Square, was among those who had been suspended.

The Amnesty Association was still at work to secure pardons for Fielden, Neebe, and Schwab. In fact, in 1891, Oglesby's successor, Governor Fifer, had seemed on the point of granting a pardon at least to Neebe. But the opposition of business leaders proved so great that he did nothing.

Now the Amnesty Association and others felt that a pardon for the three men was close at hand. Governor Altgeld read the records of the trial, but he did nothing.

[44]

All around him the controversy still surged. There remained a hard core of those who were adamantly opposed to any pardons. Some of these were prominent businessmen with much power. But public sympathy was now with the three imprisoned men. Even those who had applauded the executions seemed to feel that justice had been done, and that the punishment for Fielden, Neebe, and Schwab was too severe.

Advisers to the governor reminded him that his political career could hang on the outcome of what he did about the three men. They urged him to free Neebe and to reduce the sentences of Fielden and Schwab. (These actions, they seemed to feel, would appease everybody.) Altgeld replied that the men were guilty or not guilty — that was the issue. And if they were not guilty they must all be freed.

This was the key point for Altgeld. He could grant pardons as an "act of mercy," but he refused to do so. He would decide solely on a question of guilt.

On June 26, 1893, the governor made his decision. Samuel Fielden, Michael Schwab, and Oscar Neebe were pardoned, and set free.

As his reasons for granting the pardons, Altgeld stated firmly that the evidence at the trial had not shown the men to be guilty. He declared that the jury had been prejudiced, and that the eight men had been unjustly convicted. He ended by attacking Judge Gary for his rulings and for his handling of the trial.

The pardons were the beginning of the end for Altgeld.

It has been said that the governor was unwise in his wording of the pardons. If he had merely stated that the three men had already been punished enough, he probably would not have been so bitterly denounced. Instead, he called the whole trial a sham and attacked a respected judge. For these reasons, the pardons, instead of being generally welcomed by the public, became the excuse for a flood of bitter and heated criticism against the governor.

[45]

Altgeld was later often ridiculed in cartoons such as this.

Very few defended him. The wealthy said he was obviously a socialist. Suddenly, he was called a foreigner — even though he had lived all but the first three months of his life in the United States. The Chicago press called him unfit for the governor's chair. Newspapers in New York, Philadelphia, Detroit, and other cities condemned him and his decision.

Governor Altgeld remained silent through all the criticism, convinced that he had done his duty as he had seen it. But friends later said that he was deeply hurt by the reaction against him.

There is a difference of opinion as to how much the Haymarket pardon actually affected John Altgeld's political career. It is difficult to measure. It is true that he did not lose his reputation as an honest, dedicated man. It is true that he was renominated for governor in 1896. It is also true that he lost the election.

John Altgeld returned to private law practice until his death in March, 1902.

In all the furor surrounding the pardons, the release of Fielden, Neebe, and Schwab was little noticed. They each found a private occupation and were not heard of again in any revolutionary activities. They had spent six years in prison.

The Aftermath

The Haymarket riot remained in the minds of many people for a long time. This one seemingly insignificant affair on a rainy evening in Chicago had an impact on a large segment of the American people.

There seems little doubt that the Haymarket trial was a miscarriage of justice. It is true that the defendants advocated violence in their quest for a social revolution. It is true that they would have welcomed and participated in the overthrow of the government. Morally, at least, they were hardly blameless, yet the fact remains that the accused men did not receive a fair trial. They were not proven guilty of the charges against them. Although the Haymarket trial was not the only instance where American justice failed, it does remain a black mark on a law system that holds honor and truth as its highest ideals.

The Haymarket riot and its aftermath changed the feeling of the entire country toward radical members of society. Before the riot, most Americans either were unaware that revolutionary groups existed or regarded them in an almost amused way as being perhaps odd but certainly harmless. After the riot, revolutionaries were seen as a positive threat to the security of the United States. The effects of the country's first real red scare were long and lasting.

One of the effects was the attempt to pass laws to discriminate against anarchists and other "undesirable aliens." In 1903, an Immigration Act forbade anarchists from entering the country. In 1906 and 1907, the laws became even more rigid against them.

Revolutionary groups themselves did not stop their activities because of the Haymarket riot. However, Chicago revolutionaries did stop urging the use of force. The five men who died became the first revolutionary martyrs in the United States. Their pictures were displayed at all meeting places, and November 11 was observed as a memorial day in their honor.

Today many people believe that the May Day celebrations observed by labor movements all over the world every May 1 are a result of the Haymarket riot. This is not true. May 1 was the date set for beginning the drive for the eight-hour day, and after 1886 the day was observed for that reason.

One aspect of the Haymarket trial which remains as much of a mystery today as it was in 1886 is the identity of the bomb thrower. As we have seen, the state charged that Rudolph Schnaubelt, the young German radical, had thrown the bomb in Haymarket Square. But his guilt was never proven, one of the reasons being that Schnaubelt disappeared after the riot and was never found. And it is precisely because he did disappear that many people believe that he did throw the bomb. However, others say that his disappearance was caused by the fact that he did not wish to be given the same "justice" as the eight accused men. Whatever the case, it is said that Schnaubelt made his way to Europe, later to South America, and finally back to the United States where he died after recurring attacks of nervousness and melancholia.

However, even if the name of the bomb thrower had been definitely known (if the defendants knew it, they kept a tight secret), it would not have changed the results of the Haymarket affair. Nor would it have saved the labor movement from a setback. For labor itself suffered greatly from the Haymarket affair. It suffered in two ways — the failure of the eight-hour drive and the rise of adverse public feeling.

The Haymarket riot was not the only reason that the eight-hour drive failed. Social historians feel that the country was not yet willing to approve a shorter workday in any case. They say that labor was not yet strong enough and was too poorly organized to win its demands in 1886. Yet even if Haymarket was not the principal reason for the failure of the movement for an eight-hour day, the riot and its aftermath were seriously damaging to labor's cause. Employers could — and did — use the affair as a basis for denouncing the aims of organized labor. In 1886, over six hundred strikes were called to demand an eight-hour day. Nearly four hundred were unsuccessful. By 1896, only twelve states had granted an eight-hour day for state employees. In some cases, labor groups dropped their demands for an eight-hour day, at least partly because of the great outcry over the Haymarket riot.

The Haymarket affair became a weapon in the hands of those who opposed organized labor. It was used, in some cases most effectively, to turn public feeling against labor groups. While it cannot be said that the growth of labor unions was stopped as a result of the Haymarket affair, in many areas labor suffered from the reaction against the Haymarket riot. The riot was certainly responsible in part for many laws which were enacted to curb labor activities. These laws included severe punishments for conspiracy, and provisions for strengthening the power of the police in handling labor disputes.

The Haymarket affair is one of the many small but important

The Haymarket Affair helped to pave the way for collective bargaining instead of riots such as these.

The Haymarket monument in Chicago

episodes in the history of the United States. It has resulted in changes in laws and practices that would almost surely prevent a new version of the Haymarket riot and trial. Certainly the Supreme Court's rulings on trial procedures during the mid-twentieth century would correct the type of errors committed during the trial. And certainly the violent actions that marked the protests of the labor movement in the late nineteenth century are no longer acceptable forms of labor protest in America. Yet out of the violence of the riot and its aftermath grew the right to strike and the legitimate collective bargaining between worker and employer that are integral parts of the United States labor scene today.

INDEX